THE
Archive Photographs
SERIES

CONSETT

The Iron Works, 1840.

THE
Archive Photographs
SERIES
CONSETT

Compiled by
Derwentdale Local History Society

CHALFORD

First published 1995
Copyright © Derwentdale Local History Society, 1995

The Chalford Publishing Company
St Mary's Mill, Chalford,
Stroud, Gloucestershire, GL6 8NX

ISBN 0 7524 0336 2

Typesetting and origination by
The Chalford Publishing Company
Printed in Great Britain by
Redwood Books, Trowbridge

The world's first Salvation Army Band, formed in Consett, 1879.

Contents

Apprenticeship papers to the Society of Papermakers, 1839, in the name of John Houliston.

Introduction

For one hundred and forty years of its one hundred and fifty year history the town of Consett was a company town. It came into existence when a chance find of ironstone, combined with the availability of coal and water, prompted a small group of men to invest in the setting up of an iron and tin plate company. By the time it was realised that the supplies of ironstone were insufficient to satisfy the needs of the newly-founded works the investment was too great to pull out and arrangements were made to bring in ore from Cleveland. This commitment to the success of the venture paid dividends and a period of rapid growth began.

There were, however, insufficient local workers particularly of the skilled kind, to supply the demand that the new works were creating. Thus began the massive influx of families from other parts of Britain. They arrived with hopes of prosperity and security but were faced with hardship and inadequate living conditions. There was employment but few facilities. Even in the 1860s women would race each other a quarter of a mile to the water cart and only the lucky ones would return with water. Housing was basic and overcrowded; health was poor. Violence and drunkenness were common, not surprisingly since beer was easier to obtain than water. The comparison of the area to a frontier town in the wild west was possibly justified. However, over the years the disparate elements of the community grew together, civilising influences emerged, and the town prospered.

The development of the area and its people was always inextricably linked to the Iron Company which, as the main employer, influenced every aspect of life. It was a natural assumption in every family that, after schooldays were over, employment would be found in either the iron works or in one of the thirty-seven coal mines which were owned and run by the Company. In most cases the entire working lives of local men were spent in the same place where they had first started. Long service awards for 65 years service were commonplace. The pervasive influence of the company was extended past the workplace and into all areas of life by their provision of housing, schooling, health care and recreational facilities; they built the town.

The situation lasted till the early 1980s when the unthinkable happened, the steel works closed. The town had no experience of existing without it and a period of profound shock naturally followed. But, inevitably, life carries on and the people of Consett are now seeking a new identity. It is too early to say what shape the future will take but hopefully the grit and determination of Consett folk will surface once again to rebuild a prosperous town.

When members of the Derwentdale Local History Society were approached to make this compilation of photographs it was seen as an ideal opportunity to remind local people of their heritage, and to introduce a younger generation to aspects of their town they may never have seen. It is impossible in a work of this size to present a comprehensive picture of the area and we hope that no offence has been caused to anyone by the omission of particular subjects. The emphasis on Consett and the influence of the iron works is in no way intended to diminish the importance of the areas which pre-date 1840, Shotley Bridge and Medomsley for example, areas with a rich history of their own.

As some ex-steelworkers will know many photographs in this compilation first appeared in the Consett Iron Company magazines, which were produced over a twelve year period from 1957 onwards. We make no apologies for this, however, as we believe that they deserve to be seen by a wider audience. As far as we have been able to ascertain, the facts given in the captions to the photographs are accurate but we make no pretence to infallibility and would invite any reader to contact us if they can correct or add to the information we have given, especially in putting names to faces.

We hope that this selection of photographs will be of interest and will perhaps generate an increased awareness of our local history. The Derwentdale Local History Society is a group of local people who attempt to foster this interest by holding monthly meetings with guest speakers and arranging monthly outings around the area. New members are always welcome. We thank all those who have helped in the compilation of this book and hope that you will find it enjoyable.

Mrs Maureen Clifford
Chairperson of D.L.H.S.

This book was compiled by the following members of the D.L.H.S.:
Mrs Maureen Clifford (Hon. Chairperson)
Mr Tommy Moore (Hon. Secretary)
Mrs Norma Moore (Hon. Treasurer)
Mr David Hannen (Committee member)
Mrs Cecilia Rogan (Committee member)

One

A Glimpse at Our Surroundings

The General Offices of Consett Iron Company are on the left of this 1890 scene. The old row of workmen's houses below the Offices was Staffordshire Row, one of the earliest streets to be built in the town. Gardens, probably allotments for the nearby houses, were still in evidence and it is said that there was a farm, belonging to the Bates' family, on the site where the Works developed. This is supported by the haystack which is at the end of the row of houses, though it cannot be seen in this reproduction.

Consett Hall was one of the very few buildings in Consett to predate the formation of the iron works in the early 1840s. Now demolished, it was used for many years as the residence of high-ranking officials of the iron works, like William Jenkins. One of the managers who lived at the Hall in the mid-nineteenth century was George Forster, owner of Underhand, the region's famous racehorse.

Allansford Hall, pictured here c. 1910, was at one time the home of the Annandale family, local mill owners, who also owned the surrounding cottages and Wharnley Burn Farm.

Crook Hall was demolished many years ago. From 1794 till 1808 it provided a temporary home to a group of refugee priests from Douai, France, whilst their new college at Ushaw was being built. They had also spent some time housed in Pontop Hall at Dipton. The Crookhall estate was named in the Boldon Book as belonging to the De-la-Lay family. In 1588 it was acquired by the Shaftoes, then 50 years later the Bakers. Consett Iron Company was its last owner.

Shotley Hall was built in 1863 to replace the old hall which backed onto the river about 100 yards south of the present location. The old hall, dating from the time of Queen Anne, powered its own corn mill from the River Derwent. The present hall took seven years to build and required the diversion of a stream so that the foundations would be secure. One of its features was its many windows, over 100, of many different styles. The conservatory was demolished a few years ago because of dry rot.

11

RICHARD MURRAY HOSPITAL, BLACKHILL.

The Richard Murray hospital, built in 1912, was demolished 1992/3 to make way for a housing development. Richard Murray was a local businessman, J.P. and benefactor who donated £10,000 to provide this hospital for local residents. It was later used as a maternity hospital and then as one of the Leonard Cheshire homes for the disabled.

Opposite: The 'huts' of Shotley Bridge Hospital were built in 1939 to help cope with an expected influx of wounded troops. Near the top of the huts are vestiges of a railway platform for a spur line which was installed especially to bring the wounded to the hospital. The huts and the 'blocks' shown at the top of page 13 are due to disappear as a result of the restructuring of services in preparation for the new District Hospital at Durham.

Shotley Bridge Hospital began in 1914 as a Poor Law Institution run by Gateshead Guardians of the Poor. In 1919 it was used for war casualties and by 1926 had been acquired by Newcastle authorities as a mental hospital called the Colony. In 1939 it was again designated as an emergency hospital for war casualties. With the start of the N.H.S. in 1948 it became a General Hospital under the control of N.W. Durham Hospital Management Committee.

Blanchland, thought to be c. 1920s. The Abbey in the village was founded in 1175 by the Premonstratensian order of monks whose white habits are said to have given the village its name. Many of the surrounding small cottages were built to house lead miners.

Consett Fountain, Front Street, early this century. It was built in 1878 as a memorial to Mr Gledstone who had been instrumental in providing a water supply for the town. The fountain was the site of riots when the arrival of the Kensit preachers caused pitched battles which had to be quelled by special constables from Durham City.

Greenhead Tower, built in the 1700s, formed the entranceway to Black Hedley. The area gained its importance as an overnight stopping place for the droves of cattle en route from Scotland to the south. The cattle were often shod here, with two thin iron plates to each hoof, for protection on the long journey. Greenhead was also the birthplace of John Graham Lough, the sculptor, who gained fame in the 1820s with his huge figure of 'Milo', the Italian wrestler.

Shotley Bridge fountain was in use until the early 1950s when it was removed so that road widening and re-surfacing work could be carried out. Its whereabouts have since been uncertain.

Ritsons Road took its name from a local builder who was responsible for much of the housing in the area. The road is part of an old network of footpaths and bridleways, some dating back 300 years.

Queens Street, now known as Queens Road, Blackhill. The tree-filled area just to right of middle is now the doctors' surgery, otherwise it has remained largely unchanged.

Erected after the Great War, the Cenotaph was shown here in its original location in Aynsley Terrace. In the 1970s it was moved to the newly-constructed Civic Centre on Medomsley Road.

Looking along Wood Street, Shotley Bridge, with the gas works in the distance; now the site of Oley Meadows housing development. The gas plant began production in 1856 and ceased in 1954, when a pipeline from the Fell Coke Works was installed to bring in gas from there. Wood Street was the home of the Oley family of German swordmakers and also provided housing for many local flour mill workers.

The Barron family shown outside Swiss Cottage, Shotley Bridge. The building dates from around 1800, and has changed little in appearance since that date. At some time prior to 1860 it was the home of James Sanderson, a local doctor.

The Memorial Cottages, Shotley Bridge, were built to commemorate servicemen of the village who were killed in the Great War. Funding came from public subscription although the land was donated by the Peile family and the bricks came from the Priestman's brickworks. The cottages were rented to war veterans at a nominal sum.

A sketch of Parliament Street in its early days, when it housed some of the town's most impressive buildings. The Iron Company's Infirmary (now the Y.M.C.A.) and the Police Station were both built in the mid 1870s. On other side of the street (not shown here) was the building which housed Consett Local Board, originally set up in 1864; more recently it housed the Citizens Advice Bureau.

The Park Royal Hotel, Blackhill, was built in 1876 by Richard Murray and used as a luxury hotel. It is claimed by some that the building may have been the original Richard Murray Hospital and that nurses were seen coming and going from there, although this can not be proved. In 1961 it was acquired by Consett Iron Company and alterations were carried out to provide a home for single, graduate employees and accommodation for visitors to the Works. It now provides D.S.S. accommodation.

Bessemer Street, Blackhill, in the 1970s, demonstrated the immense, over-powering impact of the Works on surrounding residents. The lorry in the foreground was being used for clearance work after the demolition of Blackhill railway station which was underway at that time.

Derwent Cottages, demolished in the mid 1960s, had been built to house miners from nearby collieries, mainly Medomsley. The four rows of terraced houses (three rows of ten and one of twenty five) had outside toilets, tin baths hanging on the outside walls and allotments at the end of the streets. They were a safe, happy environment for the children who lived there.

LGT.14F FRONT STREET, LEADGATE

Front Street, Leadgate, in the 1960s. Other than the names of the shops the appearance of the street remains substantially unchanged.

This zoo was created at Elm Park at the turn of the century. It was well-stocked with a good variety of exotic animals to cater for the many visitors who regularly travelled into the area by train. The site was very conveniently close to the Shotley Bridge Station.

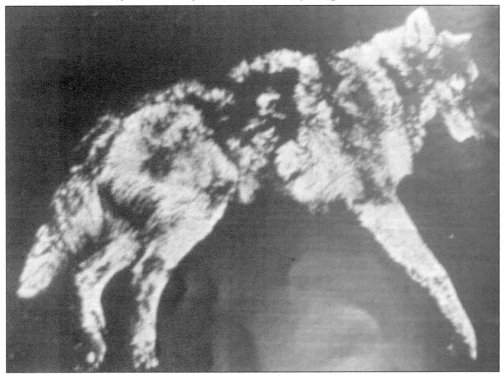

The wolf which escaped from Elm Park zoo in 1904 and managed to reach Cumwhinton before coming to grief in a collision with train. It caused much damage to sheep flocks during its spell of freedom and hunts were organised but failed to capture it. It was said to be the last wolf in England.

The band stand in the park, now the site of the car park. This view was taken from the bottom of the park and looked up towards an unfinished Aynsley Terrace. The park (called Consett park by Consett residents and Blackhill park by residents of Blackhill) was opened in 1891 by Sir David Dale. The iron company had donated the 30 acre site and borne the cost of laying out the grounds. The site was reclaimed waste land and forty to fifty workmen spent 18 months converting it to an impressive park for the use of local residents. Trees and shrubs were supplied by Robsons of Hexham who had also designed the layout.

Hownsgill Caves stone quarry was worked by the pillar and stall method of extraction which got the better quality stone from the base of the quarry without stripping off the top layers. It provided 100,000 tons of stone for the base of the nearby Hownsgill Viaduct.

Children at play on the iron bridge at Shotley Grove in 1938. The empty paper mills are in the background.

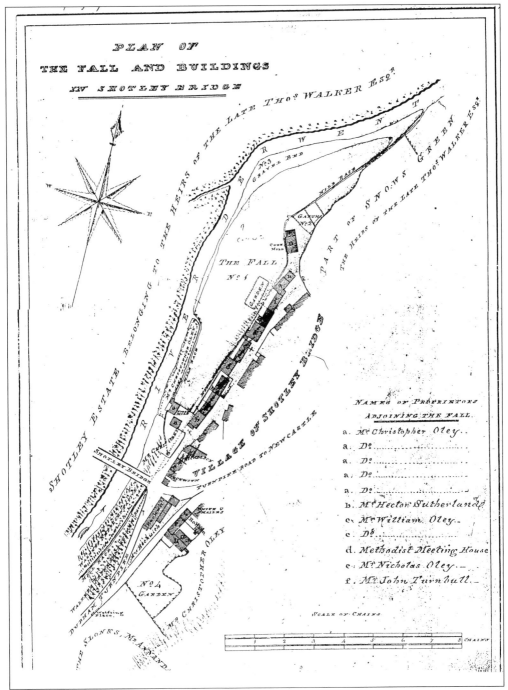

Shotley Bridge buildings and falls plan from a survey of around 1830. The main properties and buildings of the village are shown. The small lane behind the King's Head pub was already in existence and the 'low road' to Newcastle via East Law and Ebchester had just been constructed.

The bridge at Allansford was built in 1926 to replace the old single span bridge. Since then it has undergone further changes in order to cope with the heavy increase in traffic. To the left are the gates to Allansford Hall and on the far side of the bridge was the Belsay Castle Inn, formerly a religious meeting house and now converted to holiday cottages.

Allansford around the time of the First World War. The cottage was demolished when it was hit by a lorry in the early 1950s. The road is now the A68.

Wharnley Burn Bridge, Allansford, the home of Thomas Raw, the mosstrooper. At six feet nine inches in height he would sit on the hillside waiting for potential victims. He was buried under a tree at Wharnley Burn because he could not be buried in consecrated ground. It is said that the headstone from his grave is built into a barn wall at Satley but the reasons for this are unknown.

THE OLD MAN OF THE WOODS.—Thomas Thompson, a 73-year-old hermit, who lives in the Derwent Valley, near Allansford, Durham, reading a Bible while sitting in the coffin he bought 15 years ago.

Tommy Thompson, the hermit of Allansford. After being evicted from his home at Wharnley Burn, Tommy erected a wood and corrugated iron shelter at Allansford where he often slept in the coffin that he had prepared for his eventual demise. He worked for some time at the Works and it was said that when the heat of the furnaces burned the front of his trousers he would reverse them until the back, too, was burned.

This view was probably taken from the top of the Rex cinema in the 1960s and gives a panoramic view of the town centre with its industry in the background. On the right was the old bus station with its waiting rooms and toilets adjoining the car park.

The view of the steelworks from Consett's Front Street, c. 1978 with the giant gas holder and the cooling towers dominating the skyline.

The same scene seventeen years on. The reclamation of the steelworks site has provided a much greener environment where it is hoped that new sources of employment will develop.

A panoramic view from Shotleyfield, to the west of Consett. The iron company and its waste heaps show against the skyline and the housing of Bridgehill, Blackhill and Benfieldside is spread out below. At this time the Works was in full production.

Muggleswick was the vantage point for this panoramic view of the Works. The accumulation of industrial waste over several decades had a tremendous impact on the landscape and radically altered the contours of the moor land on which the town was built.

In the late 1850s a small group of local men, who were interested in providing a source of wholesome water for Consett and its surrounding areas, obtained Parliamentary powers to construct a storage reservoir to serve the needs of the burgeoning iron town. Included in this group was the same Mr Gledstone who was later commemorated by Consett fountain. By 1877 they had completed the building of Smiddy Shaw, at a cost of £86,000, with a capacity of 305 million gallons. This was inadequate even before it was completed and was supplemented by Waskerly in 1872 (450 million gallons) and Tunstall in 1879 (520 million gallons). The much larger reservoir at Burnhope was completed many years later in 1937, having been delayed because of the First World War. This photograph was taken in 1965 at the time of the construction of the Derwent reservoir which has a capacity of 50,000 megalitres. One of the hamlets submerged when the dam was filled was the picturesquely named 'Paradise'.

Consett area and the Works site in 1973 when industry dominated the town. Hownsgill Plate Mill was bottom right and the Consett to Castleside road ran diagonally across the picture, bottom left to top right.

The same scene in 1995. Demolition and reclamation work on the 680 acre site began after the closure of the steelworks in 1980. The rectangular site of the former Plate Mill is clear, bottom right. The Consett to Castleside road runs across the centre. The unfinished roads in the top half of the picture are those that will cater for the new Project Genesis development.

Two
Shops and Commerce

Victoria Road, Consett, in the 1950s, before the building of the Derwent Centre split the road into two separate areas. The Alexandra pub is visible with writing on the side wall. The buses (one Northern and one Venture) were entering the old bus station which ran parallel to Princes Street, shown behind the clock. Princes Street and Trafalgar Street, which was behind it, were the last of the old Company Rows. Both were demolished but Trafalgar Street was re-built.

The Walton Wilson brothers outside their grocery shop in Front Street, Shotley Bridge. The brothers also leased the Spa grounds around the 1880s and provided catering for up to 60,000 visitors per year, using the coal-fired oven in the basement of the shop for the baked goods.

The Refreshment Rooms, Front Street, were demolished for the building of Shotley Bridge Social Club. The small building on the right is now a betting office.

Durham Road, Blackhill, looking uphill, shortly after becoming a public road. It had formerly been a toll road owned by the Durham Palatinate who had leased it out in sections to private lessees. At this time it was still an ash surfaced road.

DURHAM ROAD, BLACKHILL, CONSETT. (17)

Durham Road, Blackhill, looking downhill, in the late 1950s. The Aberdeen granite cobbles had been left in place to help the horses climb the steep bank but they were covered with tarmac in the 1960s.

Victoria Road, Consett, thought to be in the 1920s. Behind the bus was the entrance to Atkinson & Browell's garage. Above that was the Plaza cinema. The large, open area was the site of the demolished Company Rows, later to be used as the market place. The Labour Exchange was in the background.

Consett bus station prior to its replacement by the 'bullring' station in the early 1980s. Echoes of this style, with the clock, are to be found in the new station opened in 1995.

Staff outside Clough and Pounders' grocery shop which was situated on Durham Road, opposite the bottom of Derwent Street, Blackhill.

J.R. Brodie's in Church Street, Consett, was a popular gents outfitters in the 1890s.

Middle Street, Consett, c. 1975. It was already pedestrianised and the layout has not changed but the names of some of the shops may jog some memories: Callers furniture store, Status Stores, Liptons, Jackson the Tailors and Dentons. We are told that the flat above Dentons, then housing Joan Kennedy's hairdressing salon, was the birthplace of Jimmy Saville. Jimmy's mother, Agnes, taught for a short time at the Brooms School in Leadgate.

Middle Street, 1950s. The buildings in the left foreground – the Masons Arms pub and the 'ready money' shop – were demolished to make way for the Derwent Centre. The Benefit shoe shop in the right foreground had the billiard hall above. Note the lack of traffic even though it was not yet prohibited.

Middle Street c. 1900. The tower in the distance still housed Potts' Clock. Buildings on the left have not been greatly altered, other than the shop frontages, but much of the right hand side of the street, including the Methodist Church was demolished for re-development.

Now known as part of Middle Street, this area was called Shakespeare Street 90 years ago. Consett Parish Church is in the background. On the left was the Civic Hall where popular dances were held.

The same area in the 1960s. Mortimer's outfitters, on the left, originated in Blackhill. On the right were Gibson's shoe shop, Rossi's coffee bar and Morgan's fancy goods shop.

NOTED PORK SHOP

Established in Consett in 1870

Noted for Pies, Polony and Sausages

Leave your address and our van will call.
You don't need OUR address.   It's
only the name you need and that is—

YAGER'S
THE OLD FIRM

One of the oldest established businesses in the town, Yager's is still going strong with an excellent reputation built up over many years.

The aftermath of a fire which destroyed English's shop in Middle Street. The shop front advertises 'hosiers and glovers, milliners, hatters and outfitters'. Date unknown.

Leadgate Co-operative Society was formed in 1870, although this building was not erected till 1893. The single storey building on the left was later demolished and the building was extended to its current size. Inspection these days will show that two of the upstairs windows are lower than the others, indicating where the extension work was done. The upper floor was the ballroom and there were stables blocks to the rear of the building.

Blackhill Co-op, in Derwent Street, was one of the branches of Leadgate Store. It was built in 1914 and, as well as serving the local population, it also housed the tailoring department for which the central shop in Leadgate did not have room. Its facade is now bricked up and it is owned by a local manufacturing firm.

Allendale Co-op, too, was a branch of Leadgate Store, built to cater for residents of Allendale Cottages and Medomsley. At first suitable premises could not be found and a store which had been improvised from two converted cottages was opened in 1886. By 1909 the committee were negotiating for land for a new store, and despite a clause inserted by the land owner that he would not be responsible for subsidence due to mine workings, they went ahead. This new store opened in 1911 and had to be abandoned less than ten years later – because of subsidence.

Medomsley Co-op was opened as a branch of Annfield Plain Co-op around 1890, and, because of its great success, the original building was replaced by this larger structure after only a few years. It stood near the site of Magdalene Court.

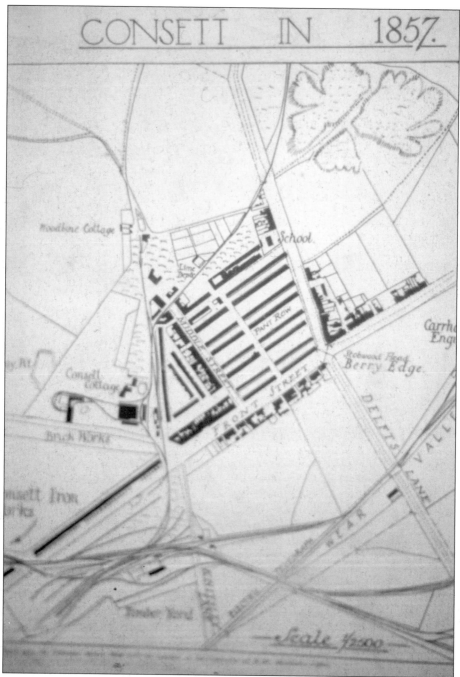

A section of the 1857 Ordnance Survey map showing Consett town centre. The rows of houses known as the Company Rows ran parallel to Front Street. They were built as basic accommodation for the iron workers who were flooding into the area at that time. They were one room up and one room down and amenities were very few. The names of the rows were later changed to Kings Street, Queens Street and Princes Street. Most of the buildings were demolished in 1924. The area has recently been re-developed with a new bus station and shops as the initial stage of Project Genesis.

The demolition of the Company Rows in 1924. The picture was probably taken from the top of the old Avenue church. The building on the corner to the left of the picture will be remembered by many as the site of Rossi's original coffee bar; many of the fittings from there went to Beamish Museum. Although there were some motor vehicles the traffic lights had not yet appeared and 'Spot' the dog was still safe enough standing near the middle of the crossroads. The demolition work was obviously popular entertainment with the onlookers.

In 1936 the site of the old Company Rows was allocated as the town's market place. This photo dates from 1960 and was possibly taken from the top of the Rex cinema.

Lambton and Co. Bank at the corner of Front Street and Victoria Road, Consett. The date is uncertain but thought to be some time prior to 1924, as the steps, bottom right, were those which led to the Company Rows which were demolished in that year.

The same site in 1965, with the more familiar name of Lloyds Bank and electric lights replacing the gas lamps. The zebra crossings have gone and the entrance has moved around the corner but this view is still very similar today.

Three
Religion and Education

Christ's Church, the parish church of Consett, was built in 1866 at a cost of £3,200. The church hall was added in 1883. It is said that the shaft of the No. 4 pit was sunk on the spot where the altar now stands. It is understood that no coal was ever mined from the shaft.

St John's Church, The Snods, was built in 1836 as the parish church for the large area around Shotley Bridge. Previously parishioners had travelled to St. Andrew's at Grey Mare's Hill.

A woodcut of Shotley Bridge Methodist Church which stood on the site of the car park beside the village hall at the end of the Terrace.

The Hopper Mausoleum at Grey Mare's Hill, built in 1752 by the Hopper family who lived at Black Hedley in Northumberland. It stands in the churchyard of St. Andrew's, a church which was re-built in 1892 but whose original structure certainly pre-dated 1680.

St. Ebba's Church, Ebchester, contains stone from the nearby Vindomora Roman fort but its date of origin is uncertain; it is said to be early Norman. At one time the Prince Bishop of Durham leased this site to the Sherburn Hospital who used it as a leper colony. This view pre-dates the restoration work which was carried out in 1876.

Rowley Baptist Church survived through times of persecution partly as a result of its remote location. Meetings began there around 1652 but the first church was not erected till around 1717. This was replaced by the present building in 1823. It is one of the oldest Baptist communities in the country and is still active.

Lanchester's All Saints is a very attractive church, parts of which date from the 13th century. In the foreground is Smallhope Burn before it was culverted under the road.

St. Aidan's Church, Blackhill, was consecrated in 1885, with the Tower and Spire added in 1904. The site was donated by Consett Iron Company and the building cost £3,676.

St. Mary Magdalene Church, Medomsley, may date back as far as the twelfth century – indicated by early grave covers found there. Also in the churchyard is a grave with the mention of a night-time burial in 1639, a measure which may have been taken to thwart body snatchers. Some Roman stones have been found in the church and these probably came from nearby Ebchester. The original flat roof was replaced with the present roof in 1878.

St. Andrew's Presbyterian Church, Durham Road, Blackhill in the 1950s. The site and much financial help toward building came from the Annandale family. It was completed in 1879 and replaced the former building in Turner Street which dated from 1860. Note the cobbled road and Bridgehill Wood above the house tops; only one tree remains visible today.

The Church of St. John the Evangelist, Castleside c. 1920s. It was built of local stone in 1867 and is a reproduction of a Swiss church.

The Wesleyan Methodist Chapel Hall, Wesley Street, c. 1900. The rubble is the remains of buildings demolished by gales – luckily they were due to be pulled down anyway. The Victoria Buildings were erected on the site. In the distance are part of the Company Rows.

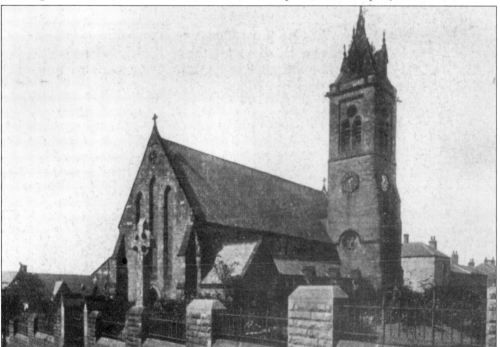

St. Mary's R.C. Church, Blackhill. Building began in 1854, soon after religious tolerance began to allow Catholics to purchase land. The building was nearing completion in 1855 when it was destroyed by storms. Unperturbed, they began again and the church was opened in 1857. On the extreme right are the now demolished Iron Company houses which included Waltons Row, West Row and Bottle Bank.

A white wedding at St. Cuthbert's, Shotley Bridge, in 1958. The church was built in 1851 from a design by John Dobson, architect of many of the classical buildings in Newcastle.

First communicants inside St. Patrick's R.C. Church, Consett, not long after its opening in 1959. It was designed by parishioner Mr Anthony Rossi and replaced the old church which had been a converted school.

Mothers waiting to collect their children from Shotley Grove School, date unknown. The school was built in 1845 by the Annandale family for 111 children of their employees, at a time when there was no state provision for schooling. It was extended (c. 1872) to cater for 173 pupils. Despite the provision of Benfieldside School in 1877, Shotley Grove School was still proving useful in 1899 when 23 boys and 25 girls were reported to be attending there. It closed completely 27 February 1903 when the last of the pupils were transferred to Benfieldside.

Benfieldside School was built as a result of the 1870 Education Act which aimed to provide a
school place for every child. In 1876 Benfieldside School Board purchased two acres of land in
Benfieldside Lane from Richard Murray at a cost of £450. They commissioned designs for a
building to accommodate 200 boys, 170 girls – to be segregated – and 130 infants. There was
also to be a master's house. On opening day, in October 1878, the master had to cope alone
with 100 boys, although the mistress did have some help to cope with the 100 girls who turned
up. Until the staffing levels improved much use was made of monitors – children of about 13

who looked after the younger ones. Absenteeism was bad, a situation made even worse by the need for parents to pay school pence which they could not afford. Around 1905 the attendance problem was improved by the appointment of the Attendance Officer – previously it had been dealt with by the caretaker! Early in 1880 the infants were moved to Derwent Street School (the Tin Mill School). Benfieldside School was altered and modernised in 1934 and re-opened with girls' and boys' departments combined. It has recently undergone extensive alteration once again.

Consett Billiard and Reading Rooms 1974, now the Steel Club. It was originally built in 1840 as a school by the Iron Company and then passed on to the British National Schools when some workers objected to paying one penny per fortnight for the upkeep of the school.

Consett Council Schools
(FORMERLY CONSETT IRON CO.'S BRITISH SCHOOLS)

Senior Boys' Department.

Awarded to William H Foreman

For General Progress in Standard III A

Easter, 1920.

Signed

Head Master.

A certificate of good progress presented from the Consett Council Schools to William Foreman in 1920. The original blast furnaces of the Works are pictured alongside more exotic locations and the wording too indicates the Company's former involvement with the school – 'formerly Consett Iron Company's British Schools'.

Pupils of Consett Church of England School in 1909 with headmaster, Mr Bertie Barrett who went for help in his horse and trap when he was the first person on the scene of the charabanc disaster on Long Close Bank.

Blackhill County Infants School, locally known as the Tin Mill School, in June 1966. On the left is headmistress Mrs D. Dunn and on the right, teacher Mrs Cleasby.

Consett Technical Institute, now the Tertiary College, was opened in 1900 to commemorate the Diamond Jubilee of Queen Victoria and also to honour the memory of William Jenkins of Consett Iron Company. Funds were raised by a combination of grants from Durham County, grants from the Consett Iron Company and public subscription. For some time in the 1960s the College used the former Medomsley Edge School as an annexe to accommodate its many students.

Four

A Night on the Town

Retired Plate Mill workers outside the Irish Democratic Club, or Demi, in the late 1950s, with steward Jimmy Clifford and his wife, Monica, middle front. Later additions and alterations to the building make it totally unrecognisable from this picture. In 1995 it became the home of Consett Rugby Club.

The opening of the Trades Union Memorial Hall in 1960. Finance for the building was raised by deduction from Iron Company workers, organised through the trades unions. The cost was £45,000 and the deductions were 2d per week.

The Burton Hotel stood on the corner of Victoria Road and Church Street, the site now occupied by the Electricity Board showroom.

Stanefordham, Moorside, near the beginning of the century.

The same scene in the 1960s. The terraced houses had become a public house, horse power had changed to motor power and the boundary wall had gone. New to the picture were the rooftops of the Moorside estate behind the pub.

The Horse and Groom, Castleside, after a snowstorm in January 1910.

The Sportsman's Arms, Leadgate c. 1920. The building stands on the site occupied by one of the first small shops opened by Leadgate Co-operative Society in 1872. Prior to this they had used a few rooms in the Golden Lion.

The Station Hotel, now the Cricketers, was built to accommodate passengers from the nearby railway station at Blackhill at a time when Blackhill was a busier centre of commerce than Consett.

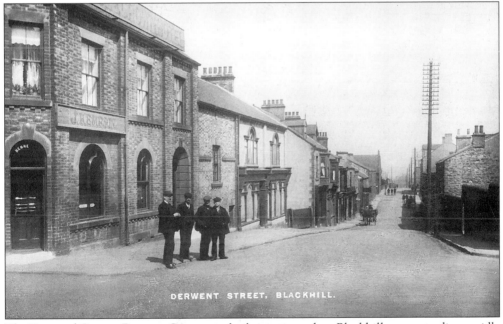

The Rose and Crown, Derwent Street, was built at a time when Blackhill was expanding rapidly because of the iron works. The growth of Derwent Street as a commercial centre was due, in part, to the fact that it was on the route of a system of footpaths which had developed from Shotley Bridge to the new industrial areas of Blackhill and Consett.

The North Eastern Hotel, Hawthorn Street, Blackhill. The pub, now demolished, was close to the railway station and was patronised by the railwaymen, as shown in this gathering of customers.

The Railway Inn, also known as the Kickin' Cuddy, on Durham Road, Blackhill. The posters in the Tap Room windows were for local theatres. It has now been converted to residential use.

Ned Gailes and his family outside the Miners Arms, Highgate Corner, Blackhill. The decorations are thought to be for the coronation of King George V in 1910.

The Bridge End Inn, the former name of the King's Head in Shotley Bridge, was the white building at the end of the bridge over the River Derwent. The Wheatsheaf Inn, in the background, was demolished when the road was widened.

Star performer with Consett Over-60s in the 1950s and 60s was seventy one year old Tommy Tilley. These were three of his guises – the cowboy, the Scotsman and the Dutchman.

Jack Little (Cost Office) who produced "Oklahoma" at Consett as the annual musical show, tells fourteen other Company employees who took part just what he wants as they sit on "the Surrey with the Fringe on the Top."

Iron Company employees rehearsed a production of the musical *Oklahoma* in 1957. Jack Little was the producer.

Pupils of Benfieldside school in their 1935 production of the operetta *The Island of Balkis*. The 'aviators', along with princes, courtiers, and medievally dressed villagers, performed the play over three nights with each performance attracting capacity crowds.

Consett Citizens Choir were the subject of a religious music programme entitled *A Steel Town Sings* which was broadcast on Sunday 16 August 1967. The musical director was William Westgarth and organist was Edward Sharp. The programme featured film taken at various sites around the area.

The Olympia, Blackhill, was built in 1912 and last used a cinema in the mid 1960s. Since then it has housed a bingo hall, a D.I.Y. shop and a joinery business.

A poster advertising performances of the *Mikado* by the local operatic group early in 1902. The venue was the Town Hall which was located at the corner of Middle Street and Front Street. The Town Hall later housed a cinema which enjoyed the local name of 'the loppy opera'. The poster mentions the supplier of the piano as being E. Sloane and Sons of the Piano Warehouse, Blackhill.

The Empire Theatre, Consett, temporarily became 'Consett's Carnival Cinema' in 1928. Attractions listed included Eddie Cantor, Kid Boots and Passions of Men. The crowds indicate the popularity of the acts.

Consett Market Square in the mid 1960s. Top right was the Rex Cinema which was burnt down in 1967. The Rex stood on the site of the old Tivoli which had also been destroyed by fire. For many years the site remained undeveloped and it has only recently been utilised with the building of the new Job Centre.

Volunteer fund-raisers for Radio Derwentside Hospital Radio, in Middle Street, Consett. The occasion was a Bumper Fun Day in June 1990. For many years Jack Padgett, a well-known local figure, was a tireless worker for the Radio Derwentside.

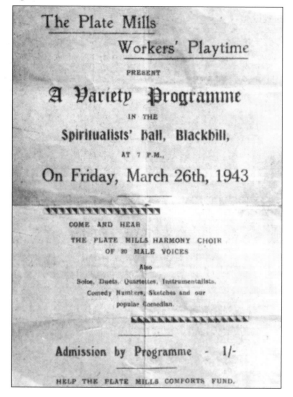

The Plate Mills

Workers' Playtime

PRESENT

A Variety Programme

IN THE

Spiritualists' hall, Blackhill,

AT 7 P.M.,

On Friday, March 26th, 1943

COME AND HEAR

THE PLATE MILLS HARMONY CHOIR
OF 20 MALE VOICES

Also

Solos, Duets, Quartettes, Instrumentalists.
Comedy Numbers, Sketches and our
popular Comedian.

Admission by Programme - 1/-

HELP THE PLATE MILLS COMFORTS FUND.

This wartime performance of the *Plate Mills Workers' Play Time* was organised in 1943 to raise money for the Comfort Funds as part of the workers' war effort.

Five
Team Spirit

Consett Volunteers set off for the Boer War c. 1905. They were marching along what was then the carriageway of Blackhill railway station; only the wall where the young boys sit remains today. The slouch hats worn by the volunteers remained in use for some years after the Boer War.

The First Consett Scouts Group, date unknown, but the clothes indicate that it may have been just after the turn of the century.

The Crookhall Volunteers, pictured here in 1907, were a fine group of young boys from that area who were trained by Bob Armstrong. Bob lived in Blue Row, Crookhall, and was himself an old soldier.

Consett Fife and Drum Band was formed in 1901 and became known as the 'whistling band'. Despite the immense popularity of the band it was forced to disband at the outbreak of war in 1914.

This Comic Band was formed by workers at the Plate Mills to celebrate victories in the Boer War.

These members of the 7th Platoon, Durham Light Infantry, were all men of the Consett area, pictured at Catterick in 1923. Names were (left to right from back); Crawford, Sculthorpe, Cant, Munroe, Parker, Greer, Hagan, Patterson, Maddison, Mannion, Ward, Pearson, Dixon, Davies, Parker, Chilton, Johnson and Johnson.

Air-raid wardens on parade past a group of dignitaries during the Second World War. The setting was Victoria Road with the old bus station roof and Princes Street in the background.

These well-posed young ladies were employed in the Despatch Office of the Works in 1917 and are an example of women playing their part in the war effort. The names were, back row: Maggie Aitken, Elsie Ramsden and Ellen Hall. Middle row: Catherine Holmes and Ella Gale. Front row: Connie Hulse and Jennie Burke.

Consett Squadron A.T.C. 1409 Squadron, in 1955, when they visited R.A.F. Swinderby in Lincolnshire. They were attending annual camp where training was carried out for national service and potential air force careers. The week's camp provided a good holiday as well as valuable training.

Blackhill Wesleyan Ladies Gymnastic Team, date unknown.

'Consett Babes', a championship-winning tug-of-war team, in 1908. Every team member worked as a metal carrier in the blast furnace bottom.

Participants of a game of cricket at Shotley Hall garden party prior to the first world war. The teams were made up of Hall servants against estate tenants.

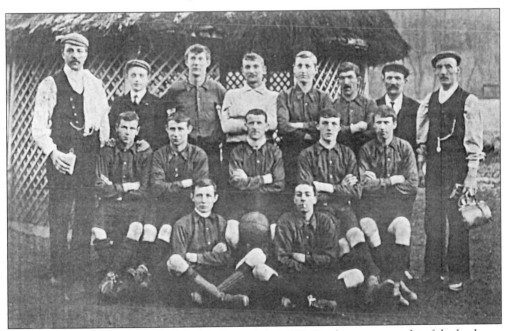

Shotley spa was the venue for this football match in 1909. On the extreme right of the back row were J. Coxon and W. Clarkson.

Dominoes have long been a popular pastime in the pubs and clubs of the area. This game took place in Consett Workmen's Club in 1957. Players were, left to right: Harry Aitchison, Tom Jones, Bill McCance and (back to camera) Paddy McAleer.

Pigeon racing has also been a firm favourite with local men for many years. Bill Robson and Norman Moss had an excellent season in 1957 with Shotley Bridge club.

Leek Club prize night was always a grand event and often involved big cash or voucher prizes, bought from funds raised throughout the whole year. These members of the C.I.C. Engineers Horticultural Society were enjoying success at their show held in the Smelters Arms, Castleside, in 1966.

The Rose and Crown darts team posed for the camera after winning the runners-up shield of the Consett and District Tuesday Night Darts League. The year is thought to be 1970. Names included: J. Watson, J. Kendall, G. Temperley, Stuart Steadman (now deceased), Ben Watson and Eric Bell.

Knitsley cricket team, 1951. Left to right, back row: Luke Brown, Gordon Bolton, Bill Johnson, Keith Sheldon, Eric Wilson, Jackie Ward. Front row; Derick Jackson, Bob Steadman, Aubrey Waller (captain), Fred Boustead and Ian Thompson.

Winners at Consett Swimming Club Gala in 1968: Susan Atkinson, Keith Walton and Joan Turley. The Amateur Swimming Club was formed in 1962 shortly after the opening of Consett Baths.

Ebchester Rowing Club members Ken Smith and Bob Bewley passed on sculling tips to interested youngsters on the banks of the River Derwent. The club was formed in the 1870s.

Underhand was bred and owned by George Forster who was manager of the iron works and lived in Consett Hall. This horse won fame and popularity by winning 14 races including the 1859 St. Ebor Handicap. His greatest achievement, however, was to win the Northumberland Plate three years running, in 1857, 1858 and 1859. This is taken from a painting by H. Hall and features, left to right: Mr. Forster, J. Forbert (trainer), A. Briggs and Aldcroft the jockey (mounted).

Bowling Pavilion, Consett & Blackhill Park.

The bowling pavilion at the bottom of Blackhill Park. The opening ceremony took place on May 16th 1923 and the club is still thriving after seventy years. The now demolished Park Road Methodist Chapel and Hall are visible in the background.

Six
High Days and Holidays

Decorations in Roger Street, Blackhill, reflected the happiness and national feeling of pride which resulted from the conclusion of the Boer War in 1901. Part of the celebrations was a march through Blackhill of the South African Militia and a display of British naval field guns. The loading of these field guns is still one of the events at military tattoos and this harks back to the Boer War when the guns used by the army were not big enough for the job in hand, and naval guns were taken onto the battlefield against the Boers. The difficult task of loading and transporting them took great strength and skill.

Consett Chamber of Trade on their annual outing, possibly in the 1930s. The motif on the bus was for Atkinson and Browell and Company who had their premises below the Plaza cinema.

Regulars from the Chelmsford, Ebchester, visited London in 1913 to attend the Sunderland v. Aston Villa cup final, where the winning goal was scored for Villa by Tommy Barber of West Stanley.

Local Licensed Victuallers, pictured outside the Commercial in Durham Road, Blackhill, preparing for their annual outing in 1910.

Campers at Coombefield in the 1920s. The area was so popular that Cowlings ran a bus service as far as Dean Howle Road Ends for the visitors. Coombefield Farm also had five chalets as well as camping facilities. Four of the eight Swainston brothers, local tradesmen, are included in this photo; Ralph Swainston, in the bow tie, ran a fish shop in Dunston.

A large gathering of St. Aidan's Mothers Union in 1954, on the church lawn. The lone male on the extreme right was Canon Beaglehole who was incumbent at St. Aidan's from 1954 till 1957. Dwindling congregations in recent years have resulted in plans for the church's closure.

Residents of Buddle Street, Consett, organised these peace celebrations following the end of the First World War. It would appear to have attracted many of the children from the surrounding area too.

Residents of Castleside on their Peace Day March in July 1919.

Consett Co-op produced this commemorative handkerchief for their 50th anniversary celebrations in 1913.

Residents of Maple Gardens, Bridgehill, on Coronation Day, 1953. There are many familiar faces in this group where party hats and a children's fancy dress competition were the order of the day.

This happy group, also depicted on the outer cover, are residents of Walton's Row, Blackhill, celebrating the Silver Jubilee of King George V and Queen Mary in May, 1935. West Row, Walton's Row and Bottle Bank, all shown in the background, were a set of basic, one-up, one-down terraced houses provided by Consett Iron Company for its workers. The houses were

demolished in the 1960s by which time they had reached an advanced state of disrepair. Known names include: Mrs Robinson, Mrs Glancy, Mrs Kearney and Mrs Murray, whose son Geordie is the young boy in the front row.

The Freemasons Hotel was the venue for this annual dinner of the Consett Iron Company garage staff in 1960. The party was obviously going with a swing. The gentleman at the front having fun with the balloon was Peter Mantle.

Consett residents Maggie and Mary Lister, George Brough and son George, and John Finnegan, at Appleby Fair in 1964. For many years the fair was considered one of the greatest horse shows.

Members of the Steel Plant Social Club, with wives and families, setting out for a day trip to South Shields in 1959.

Consett Iron Company was host to many hundreds of visiting groups who toured the site to see the steelworks in action. This group of student nurses from Shotley Bridge Hospital made their visit in the spring of 1959.

The vantage point for this view was the tower of Consett Parish Church . The buses were lined up along Parliament Street in readiness for the Poor Children's Outing in 1923. Thousands of children annually were taken to the seaside and the day was a big event in their lives.

The Market Square was the gathering point for the Poor Children's Outing in 1927. Funds were raised by Consett Volunteer Workers Association and local tradesmen were also very supportive.

The Grove and Moorside Social Club organised this trip to South Shields for 300 children and their adult companions in 1961. Each child -received five shillings spending money and competed for prizes throughout the day.

Retired workers from the Plate Mills waited for the transport for their trip to Holy Island in 1959. The trip was financed by trade union members and each of the 66 trippers also received ten shillings spending money. Retired workers were highly thought of and received very considerate treatment by the men still employed at the Works.

This Consett Iron Company tent was part of Consett Show in 1962. Earlier that year the display had also travelled to the Royal Show at Newcastle, Durham County Show at Lambton Park and to Stavanger and Bergen in Norway.

The Iron Company's travelling displays often included this scale model of the Works which helped visitors to gain an overall impression of the layout of the site.

Seven

Transport

The Venture Coach ran from Shotley Bridge to Blanchland between 1921 and 1930 then the route was changed to serve Shotley Bridge to Edmundbyers between 1930 and 1939. The service was run by Mr Lewis Priestman for his own amusement and during the season the services ran four times per week. Tickets were obtained free from Mr Priestman and a free tea was also provided. An outrider rode ahead of the coach with two grey horses which helped provide extra pulling power on the steep gradients. The teams of horses leaving Shotley were greys and these were changed at Unthank or Manor House for teams of browns or chestnuts. All of the horses had names beginning with 'V' e.g. Viking, Vanguard, Varnish, Variety, Victor etc. The coach and teams were eventually acquired by Vaux Breweries. This photo was taken in 1967 when the coach was brought for its last outing on the occasion of the Braes of Derwent Hunt, of which Mr Priestman had been an avid supporter.

The Coronation Coach is shown whilst in service but in August 1911 it was involved in a tragic accident on Long Close Bank, Medomsley. The ten passengers who died were all employees of the Co-operative Society and members of the Co-op choir. They were travelling to Prudhoe to take part in a choral competition when the charabanc went out of control after the brakes failed. At the funeral, the crowds stretched from Middle Street, Consett, to Benfieldside Cemetery.

The location was the Highgate Corner but the date can only be guessed at. The spoked wheels and solid tyres suggest its pre-dates the First World War.

Veteran of the city streets is housed in the engine sheds

In storage and in the Company's care is this veteran tram which was built in 1907 for Sheffield Corporation Tramways by the United Electric Car Company of Preston, Lancs. It has been obtained on behalf of sponsors of a museum for the North of England.

The car ran in Sheffield for over fifty years until its removal to a museum at Clapham in London.

As delivered, the tram was mounted on a Mountain and Gibson truck. It was double-deck, with a vestibule glass screen on the lower deck, but the upper deck had an open canopy. There was seating for twenty-two in the lower saloon and twenty-eight on the upper deck, with eight seats on the open canopy. In 1920 the car got a Peckham P22 truck in place of the original one. A new top deck was fitted in 1926 and the car became all enclosed. This old veteran, which carried millions of people in well over half-a-century of service to a city, is the pride and joy of our own people in whose care it has been placed.

Built in 1907, this tramcar ran for Sheffield Corporation for many years. Here it was in transit to Consett Iron Company, where it was repaired and restored, before making its way to its present home at Beamish Museum.

Not much is known about this subject but it thought to have been taken at the stables of Shotley Hall a few years before the outbreak of World War One.

Hownsgill Viaduct, built in 1857 to carry a section of the Stanhope and Tyne railway. Prior to that the rail journey had been interrupted by the ravine and freight had to be taken across it on waggons which were lowered and raised by means of a stationary steam haulage engine. For pedestrians there were 300 steps on either side.

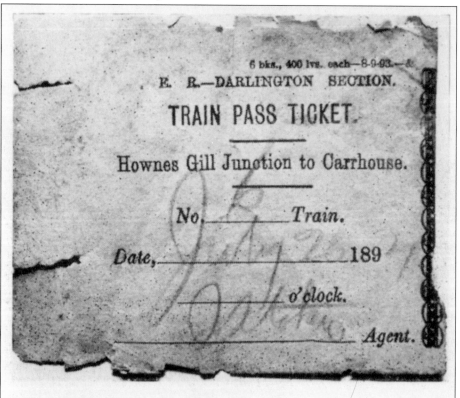

This ticket was issued 26 July 1897 for the train journey from Hownsgill Station to Carrhouse Station which was near Villa Real, Leadgate.

An early B.9 Works locomotive in 1887, with crew, left to right: John Reed, sandboy; George Burdon, fireman; William Lumsden, driver. John Reed, the sandboy in this picture, subsequently worked as a fireman, a driver and then a foreman in the Engine Sheds.

KNITSLEY VIADUCT,
LENGTH 700 FEET, HEIGHT 70 FEET, BUILT 1862.

Knitsley Viaduct, near Hurbuck, was a timber construction dating from 1862/3, built to carry the railway. When it was found to be unsafe it was not dismantled but instead was in-filled with ballast to form embankments. It is still possible to walk across the top of the old railway line.

This guardsman at Leadgate Station was giving the signal for the train to leave for Consett. The Commercial Hotel is in the background. The railway line is now part of the Sustrans cycle path from Consett to Sunderland.

Winter 1909 at Rowley Station. The station, which dated from 1867, was dismantled and rebuilt at Beamish North of England Museum where it is one of the most popular attractions.

Staff of Blackhill Station. Many railway photographs of this era show these wicker baskets standing on station platforms and metal milk churns, too, were a common sight. The standing worker on the right is believed to be Mr Patterson.

Blackhill railway station shortly before demolition in the late 1960s. It is said that on one day each year the gates to the railway bridge were padlocked shut and that the first person to ask admission was required to pay a toll of one penny in order to maintain the rights of the railway station as a private venture and not a public right of way.

This giant transformer was on its return trip to the Works after having repair work completed at English Electric in 1966. The transporter belonged to local haulier Siddle Cook who also founded the very successful firm which produced Elddis caravans.

Leadgate crossroads was the setting for this test of driving ability in 1966. The lorry was carrying a girder weighing 57 tons and measuring 87 feet in length. It was part of a 200 ton crane being installed at the Oxygen Plant.

In 1958 the Works took delivery of its new ambulance, shown here on the right, with its predecessor of 23 years service on the left. The importance of health and safety to the management of the Works was apparent as early as 1876 when they set up an infirmary in Parliament Street, now the Y.M.C.A.

One of the many vehicles used by Consett Iron Company to deliver coal and other wares around the area. The solid tyres indicate the date to be pre-World War One.

The S.S. *Knitsley* was one of a number of ore-carriers owned by the Company, all of which bore local names. Others were the S.S. *Iveston*, S.S. *Leadgate*, S.S. *Consett*, S.S. *Garesfield* and S.S. *Blackhill*.

The launch of the Empress of Canada, built on the Tyne, in 1961. 1,000 tons of Consett steel were used in the vessel which was commissioned as the flagship of the Canadian Pacific fleet.

Eight
Working Life

H.M.S. *Resolution*, the first Polaris submarine, after being accepted into service in the mid 1960s. These vessels carried sixteen Type A3 Polaris missiles as well as a conventional torpedo armament. Each missile was 31 feet long, with a range of 2,500 nautical miles, with computer-controlled targeting and launching. The submarines themselves were powered by pressurised water nuclear reactors. These factors, along with the ability to stay submerged and be self-supporting for long periods of time, made the Polaris submarines the most advanced vessels of their type at that time. Consett had a special interest in these vessels, which were made by Vickers Ltd., because the Works had supplied 5,000 tons of low alloy 'Q.T. 35' steel which were used in their manufacture.

The picturesque Lead Mill Cottage in the Derwent Valley is located in an area of lime kilns, quarries and ore mines but there is no evidence, other than its name, that it was directly linked to a lead mill. Very little has changed since this was taken in Edwardian times other than the iron and concrete footbridge which now replaces the wooden structure, bottom left. The notices on either side of the cottage doors may indicate that the cottagers sold refreshments there.

The corn mill at the top of Barley Mill Road, Bridgehill, was built by the Annandale family. At one time Beamish Museum expressed an interest in re-building the mill at the museum site but the cost was prohibitive and the building was demolished.

Shotley Grove paper mills were the property of the Annandale family who had many business interests in the area. The land was purchased in 1812 and a small mill, producing hand-made paper was set up. It was later mechanised and by 1882 it was producing 40 to 50 tons per week of various types of paper, including that used for shirt collars and cuffs.

The first iron-clad blast furnaces at Consett were designed and built by a Mr Cuthbertson. This type of furnace was notoriously difficult because they had to be charged from the top. After the iron ore had been pushed manually, by wheelbarrow, up the very steep incline at the side of the furnace, it was tipped into the blast top. The parapets around the top of the structures were for the safety of the labourers who did this dangerous and exhausting work.

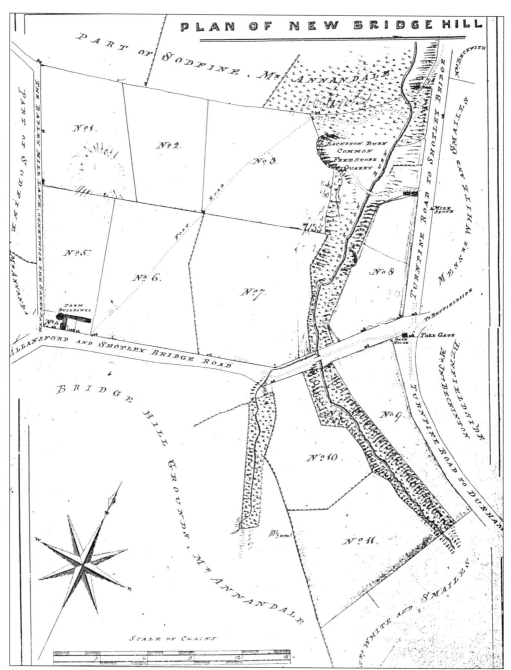

This plan of New Bridgehill was one part of a compilation of the Annandale estates, 1829. The set of maps was part of a private survey carried out by the Annandale family of Shotley Grove who owned large tracts of land in the area. As well as having many, wide-ranging business interests – from farming to mill owning – they were also involved in all aspects of community life; they served on local school boards, local governments boards and numerous committees, as well as being philanthropic in their donations of cash and land for local projects like the building of St. Andrews Church. This particular section of the survey demonstrates the sparse population of the area before the iron works started to exert its influence.

Nicholas Oley, the last member of the Oley family of German swordmakers, whose decision to settle in Shotley Bridge in the late 17th century was probably a crucial factor in the foundation of an iron industry at Consett.

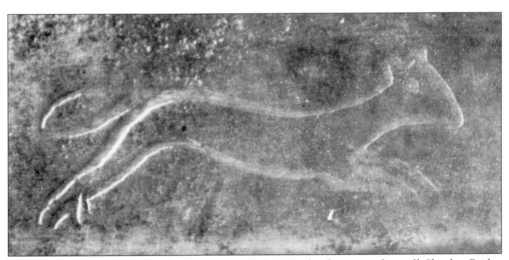

The Passau wolf, or running fox as it was called in England, was used on all Shotley Bridge swords although it originated in Solingen, Germany. Many Shotley swords were produced for the personal use of King James I and his courtiers. Their quality was also recognised in the quote from Shakespeare's 'Henry VIII' which reads 'We shall spit them on our English foxes'. The reference to 'them' was to the French who were at war with England at the time.

Chopwell colliery was one of 37 owned by Consett Iron Company. Of particular interest here is the row of beehive ovens which were used to convert small coal into coke.

These two miners worked at Medomsley pit and are thought to be pictured around 1920. The man sitting is J.Fairlamb.

Eight Men and Boys who LOST THEIR LIVES

AT THE BUSTY PIT MEDOMSLEY, NEAR CONSETT,

Which occurred on Saturday February 24th., 1923.

And as an expression of Sympathy for the bereaved Families.

THOMAS CANT, (48) Ledgate.   JAMES HORNSBY, (31) Consett.
THOMAS Wm. THORBURN (16) Consett.   DENIS O'NEIL (17) ,,
CLARENCE PAYNE (17) Consett.   FRANCIS O'HANLON (18) ,,
CHARLES Anthony COOPER (16) Consett. JAMES SMITH (17) B'khill.

They left their homes in perfect health,
And little thought of death so nigh.
But God thought fit to take them home
And with his will we must comply.

'Tis hard to part with those we love,
Tho' parting days will come,
Yet let us hope to meet again,
In heaven with the ones we loved.

A commemorative card containing the names of the eight miners killed at the Busty pit, Medomsley, on 24 February 1923. A cage, filled with the eight miners, was ascending the shaft when something caused it to become detached and fall back down. It became wedged and the occupants were thrown to their deaths. Six of the miners were still in their teens.

As late as the 1950s there were still very young men going down the pits. This young miner, Peter Clifford, was setting off from his home at Derwent Cottages for his first day down the Busty pit. The year was 1954 and Peter was fourteen years old.

Charging an L.D. furnace in the Basic Oxygen Steel Plant. The charge of molten iron and scrap amounting to perhaps 140 tonnes would then be reduced to high grade steel in about 45 minutes.

Teeming a cast of steel. The product of high grade molten steel, after being tapped into a steel ladle, was then teemed into ingot moulds by Casting Bay men, seen here on a typical cast.

This steel transporting 'torpedo train' was used to import molten iron the 56 miles from Teeside to Consett because of exceptionally high production demand. The first trip was made in August 1969 – the longest distance attempted with the torpedo system to that date.

No. 1 Blast Furnace, 1978. Consett had three blast furnaces, any two of which were likely to be in production at any one time. Production demands could reach as high as 21,000 tonnes of molten iron per week.

JOINT UNION COORDINATING COMMITTEE

SAVE CONSETT STEEL CAMPAIGN

Town on

the march

Part of the unsuccessful campaign to save Consett Iron Company was this march through the town in 1980. Although the workers fought hard to reverse the closure decision by arguing the case for the viability of the Works the outcome was already determined.

Nine

Familiar Faces

'THE PONY GIRL'

Ella Charlton was a keen animal lover and, as a member of the R.S.P.C.A., was instrumental in setting up animal welfare in the Consett area. Her interest in animals began in her father's smithy. She was also a Cub Master with the Boy Scouts and a hospital visitor. Most of her 47 years with Consett Iron Company were spent working in the telephone exchange but in her early days she was the only girl despatch rider, making deliveries on horseback. She is shown here with Queenie, a horse which was bought from a Consett publican after it had bolted with a trap.

A farmer with his pipe after his day's work was done. It is thought to be Mr Oliver Lowery of Coombefield House.

Little is known of the location of this photograph but it is certainly local. The pipe smoker in the back row is thought to be Nicholas Oley, the last member of the Oley family of German swordmakers.

Washing day in Back Albert Road, Consett, 1963. The accepted practice of stringing the clothes line across the back lane has almost disappeared because of the increase in car ownership.

Sister and brother, Kathleen and Vincent McKenna outside their home in St. Mary's Street, Blackhill, in the early 1950s.

John McKean, a founder member of Blackhill Comrades Club, served on the committee there for many years.

P.C. 804, Alf Stephenson, who was one of the area's last 'old time bobbies', was stationed at Deneburn Terrace, The Grove, from 1935 till his retirement in 1946. He often confiscated the sledges of the local children if he found them straying too near the main bus route; they were returned after a day or two with the warning that they would be chopped up if it happened again.

One of the early 'iron masters' of the area was Sir David Dale who was associated with the Consett iron industry for over 50 years, from 1854 till his death in 1906.

William Jenkins, bearded, centre front, was a Welshman who came to Consett from the Dowlais Iron Company. He was General Manager for many years and was active in community life outside of the Works, serving with local government and on many committees.

Prince Charles, on one of his visits to Consett in 1982, was given the opportunity to examine a rare example of a Shotley Bridge sword. With the Prince was Sir Charles Villiers, Chairman of British Steel.

Another royal visitor to the Works was the Princess Royal. She was accompanied by Viscount Ridley on the trip in 1962 and was here pictured at the main entrance to the General Offices.

The now-celebrated actor Alun
Armstrong, aged 17, taking the leading
role in Consett Grammar School's 1964
production of *Hamlet*. Janice Maddison
was Ophelia and Muriel Batey was
Gertrude.

Local singer Susan Maughan, known for
her successful recording of 'Bobby's Girl' in
the early 1960s, took the opportunity to
chat to a locomotive driver during her
informal visit to the steel works.

A crowd of 20,000 people lined the streets of Shotley Bridge in June 1967 when the Braes of Derwent Supporters Club organised a meet in the County Fair. These spectators were watching the last outing of the yellow and maroon Venture Coach, which set out from Shotley Hall to travel, via the King's Head, to the Spa Grounds where a crowd of 5,000 people were waiting. One villager amused the watching crowds by performing a Dick Turpin act on the passengers of the coach, who were made up of local personalities. Onlookers were also entertained by brass bands, mounted police displays and many other events.

Members of the Derwentdale Local History Society on one of their regular monthly outings. The venue on this occasion was Durham Castle.

Acknowledgements

Whilst every effort has been made to contact and acknowledge due copyright within this book, the Derwentdale Local History Society would like to acknowledge and thank those copyright holders of photographs contained within the publication where this has not been possible. Acknowledgement is offered to (by alphabet):

Mr Eric Bell, British Steels, General Steels Record Office,
Cambridge University, Library Section, and Dr Mark Nicholls in particular,
Mrs V. Carruthers, Mr R. Coombes, Derwentside District Council, Mr and Mrs Dale,
Mr John Dodd, Mr John Gailes, Dr J. Hamilton, Mr Ian Heslop, Mrs J. Hodgson,
Jefferson Air Photography Ltd., Mrs Maureen Ledger, the Library Section, the *Northern Echo*,
North East Water, Vickers plc., Mr Bill Stafford, Mr Tom Stephenson, Mr Aubrey Waller,
Mr Les Winter